Preach
Weddings

Rod Symmons
Tutor in Applied Theology, Trinity College Bristol
Vicar of Redland Parish Church

GROVE BOOKS LIMITED
RIDLEY HALL RD   CAMBRIDGE   CB3 9HU

Contents

1   Just 'A Few Words from the Minister'?.. 3

2   The Changing Patterns of Marriage 5

3   The Changing Provisions of the Church 8

4   What's the Good of Marriage? 12

5   Preach it like Beckham! 15

6   Some Ideas Based on Specific Readings 22

     Appendix 27

     Notes 28

To Beth, with thanks for sharing the adventure that is marriage.

The Cover Illustration is by Peter Ashton

First Impression September 2005
ISSN 0144-171X
ISBN 1 85174 602 1

Just 'A Few Words from the Minister'?

1

Give a minister a good meal and a few glasses of wine and the chances are that the conversation will turn to 'weddings I have known.'

Those of us who conduct them have all got good stories to tell—of the car that broke down on the way to the wedding, or the dog dressed as a page-boy that slipped its lead in the churchyard.

Amidst these tales of the unexpected, however, perhaps the thing that has surprised me most is how often people say that one of the things they most remember about their wedding was the address. Sometimes I have been left floundering to recall a talk that I have long forgotten, but which obviously lives on in their memories. Contrary to the prejudices of some clergy who hold that preaching is redundant on such occasions, these experiences suggest that a well-crafted sermon can make a huge impact on both the couple and their guests. This in turn serves as an incentive to make our preaching at weddings as creative and effective as possible.

These experiences suggest that a well-crafted sermon can make a huge impact on both the couple and their guests

In the first part of Cranmer's marriage service there was no provision for readings or a sermon because he intended that the ceremony would lead into a celebration of Holy Communion, complete with readings and an address. This provision echoed the earlier recommendation of Tertullian that the marriage ceremony should take place in the context of Communion. In practice, this seldom happened and so the rubrics of the *Book of Common Prayer* state that the minister should either read a selection of pertinent New Testament texts on the duties of husbands and wives, or should preach a sermon. Again, this was by no means universally observed. In *Common Worship*, the Ministry of the Word is mandatory—there must be a Collect, at least one biblical reading and an address.[1]

The Grove series last explored this topic in the wake of the last round of liturgical revision which culminated with the publication of the ASB in 1980. Much of what Ian Bunting said in his booklet at the time is still of great value, but the publication of *Common Worship*, coupled with the enormous social changes that have taken place in the last 25 years, suggests that it is time for a fresh look at this task.

Although I refer mainly to Anglican wedding services, it is hoped that this booklet will be of value to readers beyond the confines of the Church of England. Whilst specific applications are made to this Church, the issues raised and the principles behind them apply to other denominations and to churches in other parts of the world.

The Changing Patterns of Marriage 2

In 1980, when Ian Bunting wrote his Grove booklet on Preaching at Weddings, 68% of all first marriages took place in the context of a religious ceremony.[2]

Between 1975 and 1994, the proportions for all marriages in England and Wales were stable, evenly shared between religious and civil ceremonies (never less than 47.5% nor more than 52.5%)[3]. Wesley Carr commented on the sometimes superficial reasons why people chose a religious ceremony—flowers, space, photographs and music.[4]

The proportion of religious ceremonies amongst all weddings had fallen to just 32%

The situation in England since then has changed enormously. Churches no longer have the monopoly on elegant buildings and photogenic locations. While the Anglican church managed to increase its 'market share' of religious weddings in the final decade of the last century very slightly (from 66% to 67%), it did so against the backdrop of a very rapidly diminishing market. By 2003, the proportion of religious ceremonies amongst all weddings had fallen to just 32%, with Anglican weddings in England and Wales dropping from 348,000 in 1990 to 231,000 in 2002.

For anybody who believes that the church has something important to offer to couples getting married, these are depressing statistics. The reasons for this decline are not hard to find.

Poor Practice in the Past

In the days when the church had a virtual monopoly on weddings, it was quite clear that many clergy found weddings to be something of an irritation. In some town-centre churches it was not uncommon for there to be three or four weddings each Saturday and couples often felt as if they were on a conveyor belt. Little care was taken over preparation, and stories of clergy forgetting the names of the bride and groom proliferated.

The Effect of Greater Choice

The 1994 Marriage Act represented a momentous change in the regulations surrounding marriage in England and Wales, the most significant piece of legislation since civil marriage was introduced in 1836. It offered two important new choices to couples wanting to get married. The first, introduced in January 1995, enabled couples to get married at a Register Office other than the one in the district where they lived. Overall, however, weddings in Register Offices have fallen from 152,994 (54% of all weddings) in 1995 to 108,240 (40%) in 2003. It was the second new option, of 'approved premises' for civil ceremonies, that has made the most impact. This enabled hotels, stately houses and other locations to apply for permission to host marriages. Since most of these are able to provide attractive settings for the reception, and in many cases can also offer overnight accommodation to wedding guests, they are becoming venues of choice for those who can afford them. Weddings in approved premises grew rapidly from 2,496 (0.9%) in 1995 to 73,340 (27% of all weddings) in 2003. This choice will increase further when people rather than buildings are registered and couples are allowed to marry in many more places so long as they have a licensed registrar prepared to conduct the ceremony.

No reliable statistics are kept officially of weddings of English and Welsh residents held overseas, but Mintel estimates that these represented an additional 30,000 weddings in 2003, roughly 10% of the total weddings 'market,' a proportion that is growing steadily each year.[5]

The General Marginalization of Christianity

Whether one dates the demise of the 'Christian consensus' to the 1960s,[6] or to the decline in church attendance that started in 1904, the fact remains that church affiliation is very much a minority option in contemporary Britain. Anglican attendance fell by 5% in the 1980s and by 14% in the 1990s. The equivalent figures for children were 17% and 28% respectively. This means that the generation now approaching marriage is far less likely to have had a church connection in their youth than their parents and grandparents, and consequently they are much less likely to consider getting married in church.

The Increasing Prevalence of Co-habitation

When I was first ordained in 1983 I can recall a couple coming to see me about having their banns read. They handed me the form, and then looked to see how I would react to the fact that they had entered the same address on the form. They knew, and I knew, that this was not the way it was supposed to be. Twenty years later this is simply not an issue. Different addresses on the form are now a rarity (and may, in fact, represent no more than one partner moving out of a shared home to satisfy the residency requirements for the marriage).

In the 1950s just under 2% of couples lived together before marriage. This increased to around 5% during the 1960s, but by 1996 76% of women reported that they had lived with their first husbands before marrying.[7] This figure rises to 86% for those approaching a second marriage.[8] While most couples in their first cohabiting union still say that they expect to marry their partners eventually, the proportion is declining, and those who do marry are much more likely to do so in a civil ceremony than a religious one. The proportion of non-married women aged between 18 and 49 who were cohabiting increased from 11% in 1979 to 29% in 2002.[9]

The good news inherent in all these changes is that those who desire to get married in church are no longer requesting the default option. They have already taken two positive decisions, the first to get married at all and the second to do so in church rather than some other venue. The very least that we can do is to welcome them and, in the case of Anglican churches, help them through the anachronistic legal jungle that still surrounds ecclesiastical marriage.

Assuming we can navigate the legal preliminaries, we are then in the position to start to help them to plan a wedding in which they are able to express their commitment to each other in the context of a Christian service.

3

The Changing Provisions of the Church

A New Service

During the period of consultation leading up to the publication of *Common Worship*, there was considerable discussion about a radically different alternative form of service for marriage, but in the event what was published bears a very close resemblance to the provisions of the *Alternative Service Book* that it replaced.[10]

As with other Pastoral Services, there is a range of material designed to fit a variety of personal circumstances—not just of the couple, but of their extended families.

The guiding principle of the new Pastoral Services has been the idea of 'staged rites,' which recognizes that the great events that shape our lives do not happen out of the blue. They are generally part of a longer 'journey' or process, that needs to have some liturgical recognition.

In the marriage service, the concept of staged rites is most evident in the intentional separation of the Declarations and the Vows. In the ASB there were a number of possible positions for the Ministry of the Word, but on most occasions it happened *after* the completion of the marriage ceremony. In *Common Worship* this remains an option, but the expectation is that the sermon will come between the Declarations and the Vows. The liturgical effect of this is to separate the Declarations, which are in effect a formalization of the engagement, from the Vows, which represent the making of the marriage.

I must admit that when I first saw this suggestion, I could not imagine that it would work—would the bridal party who had just made their way into position really be prepared to push the 'pause' button on the ceremony and return to their seats for the readings and address? Against these instincts, I have offered the choice to all the couples that I have married since the book was introduced and, to my surprise, an increasing number have opted for the new provision.

There are choreographic and logistic implications to locating the Ministry of the Word in this position, but there are also serious implications for the preacher. A sermon preached after the marriage has been declared and blessed has an element of celebration. It will speak of the meaning of the commitment that has already been made and an adventure in marriage that has just begun. A sermon preached between the Declarations and the Vows has more of a commentary feel about it, exploring the meaning of the step that the couple have just committed themselves to take.

It is impossible to prepare a wedding address adequately without knowing in advance whereabouts in the service the address is to take place

It is impossible to prepare a wedding address adequately without knowing in advance whereabouts in the service the address is to take place.

A New Approach to Remarriage

The Church of England, along with other denominations, has long been exercised about the question of whether or not someone who has previously been married to a partner who is still alive should be married in church. In 1971, *Marriage, Divorce and the Church* (The Root Report) recommended circumstances in which second and subsequent marriages would be permitted in church. The report was given a rough ride in the subsequent debates in General Synod and the failure to reach agreement led to further commissions and eventually to different policies being implemented in different dioceses and parishes.

The widely adopted 'compromise' solution was to allow the couple to be married in a civil ceremony and for a service in church to follow this marriage. This was intended as a way of honouring both the principle of the permanence of marriage and the idea that the Christian faith is open to the possibility of failure and fresh starts.

This service, which was properly termed 'A Service in Church to Follow Civil Marriage,' was almost universally referred to as a 'Blessing Service' and, however hard clergy tried to explain the situation, had the effect of making the church appear hypocritical. The message communicated was that the church did not approve of remarriage, but if you went off and did it somewhere else, the church would then bless something it did not really approve of. Increasingly the situation broke down, and by 1996 nearly 10% of marriages in the Church of England and Church in Wales involved one or more divorced persons.[11]

The report commissioned by the House of Bishops, *Marriage in Church after Divorce*, which was published in 2000, sought to bring some kind of national consensus to the situation to try to end the 'postcode lottery' that was the experience of couples seeking remarriage in church. The guidelines included in the report are sensible and provide a good framework for a minister to explore with a couple the legacy of the previous relationship or relationships.[12]

9

What the report does not consider is the fact that there are parallels to many of these concerns with couples who may not have been previously married, but may have been in long-term cohabiting relationships that have broken down. Our apparent preoccupation with marriage has too often given the impression that the church views these other relationships as unimportant and that the responsibilities taken on with them—especially those involving children—do not matter. I think of one man who left his partner and their children and began a relationship with another woman from a neighbouring village. Their legal status as 'bachelor' and 'spinster' enabled them to be married in church within a matter of weeks, and no reference was made to the deserted family.

The Implications for the Minister and the Preacher

The new services, the new arrangements for the remarriage of divorced persons, and the prevalence of cohabitation all call for a great deal more flexibility and realism in the conduct of marriage in church. The implicit assumption of traditional liturgies has been that the bride and groom leave their parental homes on the morning of their marriage and establish a new home with one another after the ceremony. This is now a reality in only a minority of cases, and it is important for the marriage service to reflect the truth of what is actually taking place. *Common Worship*, for example, provides the opportunity for the bride and groom to enter the church together, and this may well be something that cohabiting couples feel better fits their situation.

In preparing the address, the preacher will need to consider whether reference should be made to the previous relationship

In preparing the address, the preacher will need to consider whether reference should be made to the previous relationship. Circumstances vary on this, and the consideration is by no means confined to divorce—the same care needs to be taken where one or both of the partners has been widowed or suffered the breakdown of a long term cohabiting relationship.

Where there are children involved it is imperative that they are acknowledged in the address and in other parts of the service—especially the prayers. The establishment of the new marriage is a very significant moment in their lives as well as in the life of the couple, and they need to be supported and affirmed.

Where there are no children, it is still wise to make some reference to the previous relationship. I recall one wedding that I attended where one of the partners had been bereaved after only a few years of marriage. Many of the guests had been at the previous marriage, yet no mention was made of the partner who had died or of their family at what must have been a particularly poignant and painful time for them. By contrast, I recently attended a wedding of a friend who was marrying a divorcee. In the course of the address a brief mention was made to the breakdown of the earlier marriage. The address did not dwell on it, but there was a connection made with something that everybody present knew was part of the reality of the new marriage.

There is a clear interplay here between the roles of pastor and preacher

These are delicate matters and it is important that the preacher should discuss beforehand with the couple what approach they think would be appropriate in the context of the wedding. Often I have found it best to give the couple the opportunity to go away and talk through the issues together, and where appropriate to consult their children or other family members, before meeting up again to decide the best way forward.

There is a clear interplay here between the roles of pastor and preacher. There will be many matters that come up in the conversations leading up to a marriage that it would be inappropriate to refer to in the context of the wedding address, but what is said in the address should have a sense of honesty and integrity that reflects the reality of the circumstances of the marriage.

4 What's the Good of Marriage?

As we have already seen, the public's understanding of marriage has changed enormously over the last half century.

There is little indication that there is any emerging consensus on the role that marriage will play in the twenty first century.

The diversity of different views about marriage will be reflected within the congregation and the sensitive preacher will want to give some thought to how to speak into this situation. Apart from any other purpose it may serve, the address needs to provide a gentle apologetic for the Christian vision of marriage. If this is done effectively it will in turn provide an apologetic for the Christian faith itself.

Those who listened attentively to the earlier part of the service will have learnt that marriage was given by God so that a man and woman can grow together in love and trust, express that love through 'the delight and tenderness of sexual union' and offer their children a secure environment in which to be born and nurtured.[13]

This represents a significant change of priorities from the order in which Cranmer set out the three causes for which matrimony was ordained: the procreation of children; a remedy against sin; and 'the mutual society, help and comfort' that the parties ought to have for one another.[14]

The compilers of *Common Worship*, like Cranmer before them, have drawn on the insights of Augustine of Hippo, who remains one of the most influential Christian thinkers on the institution of marriage. Augustine wrote his treatise *On the Good of Marriage* in the face of two conflicting contemporary views.[15] On one side were the Manichees, a religious group with which Augustine himself was associated before his conversion, who saw human souls as sparks of light trapped in material bodies. They advocated abstention from reproductive intercourse. On the other side were those who held to the old pagan Roman view that marriage was primarily an economic and political arrangement and was not the exclusive outlet for sexual relationships.

If few people today would side with the Manichees, it is striking that many modern views of marriage bear more than a passing resemblance to those held by the ancient Romans. Augustine's response therefore bears some reflection by those who bear the responsibility of being advocates for marriage in a culture that has little understanding of the distinctive purpose of this institution.

In summary, Augustine highlighted three 'goods' of marriage: procreation (although this was not the limit of his understanding of the benefits of sexual relationships), fidelity and permanence. Although Augustine expressed this third 'good' in terms of a sacramental understanding of marriage that was rejected by the Reformers, the importance of seeing marriage as a life-long commitment remains at the heart of all orthodox understandings of marriage.

Each of Augustine's 'goods' of marriage is undervalued in contemporary western culture

Each of Augustine's 'goods' is undervalued in contemporary western culture. It is not just cohabitation and promiscuity that have weakened traditional understandings of marriage, but the prevalence amongst 'respectable' (and, in North America particularly, church-going people) of what has become known as serial monogamy.

One model that has shaped my own thinking, and preaching, has been that offered by the writers Jack and Judith Balswick. On reflecting on the lack of good role models for marriage and family in the Scriptures, the Balswicks identified four theological principles for healthy family relationships: unconditional love, forgiveness, empowerment and intimacy.[16]

These can be represented diagrammatically as a 'virtuous circle':

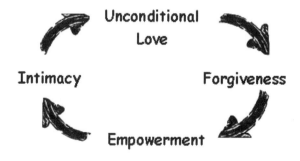

Figure 1: A healthy family structure

The idea of the circle is that each of these characteristics feeds into the next. The model can be better understood if we also consider what happens when these qualities are missing from a relationship. What results can be seen as a 'vicious circle':

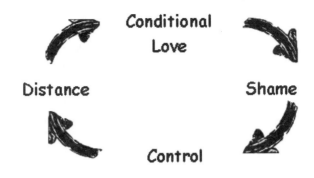

Conditional Love

Distance

Shame

Control

Figure 2: A hurting family structure

The contrast between unconditional and conditional love can be thought of in terms of the difference between covenant and contract. In the case of contract, love is dependent on the performance of the partner. This is manifest at the lower part of the circle in the way in which power is used in a relationship, either to serve a partner and bring out the best in that person or to use that power in a manipulative and controlling manner.

Ultimately any individual or couple would say that their goal in the relationship is to achieve intimacy. This model explains why some couples find it whilst others find a growing distance opening up between them. The Balswicks are not suggesting that any given relationship will be exclusively 'healthy' or 'hurting'—even relatively healthy relationships will have periods when they slip into destructive patterns of behaviour—but they are saying that there are choices that individuals make about the basis on which they want their relationship to function.

This model of loving and being loved, forgiving and being forgiven, serving and being served, knowing and being known, is one that any thoughtful person can see works out in practice in the relationships that they know. For the preacher, there are of course some very big theological themes that lie behind each of these ideas. Above all, we know that the model is not just theoretical—we see it in action in the relationship that God has established with his people, and has been demonstrated in practice in the person of Jesus.

It may seem to be labouring the point to include this discussion in a book on preaching at weddings. But the purpose of the sermon is not just to comment on the love that the couple have for one another, or to offer some helpful tips for successful marriages. Our primary aim must be to set forth a vision of the biblical view of marriage. We can only do this if we are able to fit the specific insights from the particular passage on which we are speaking into the bigger picture of Christian teaching on marriage.

Preach it like Beckham! 4

Back in October 2001, with just a few moments to go, a very nervous England football team were a goal down against Greece, in a vital qualifying match at Old Trafford.

David Beckham stepped up to take a free kick on the edge of the penalty area and floated a perfectly taken kick into the top corner of the net, booking England's place at the World Cup Finals in Japan. Sitting at home it all looked so easy, but the truth of Beckham's lethal right foot was practice—the hours spent on the training ground, working away so that he knew exactly what he was going to do when the moment came.

Odd as it may seem, the superstars of the first century world were not footballers or pop idols but public speakers. 'Rhetoric' may be a pejorative term today, but in the ancient world it was a highly valued skill—one which was practised every bit as diligently as David Beckham approaches the business of taking free kicks. If we wish to communicate effectively as preachers, not least at weddings, we could do worse than study five basic elements of classical rhetoric that they worked so hard on.

Invention

This is the first stage of any public speaking—discovering what there is to say. The title does not suggest that you just 'make it up,' although listening to some preachers I sometimes wonder if they think that originality is all that counts and that somehow to have engaged in some reflective reading in preparation for an address is cheating.

The Second Helvetic Confession sets out an astonishing, and humbling, vision for the preacher: *Praedicatio verbi dei est verbum dei*—the preaching of the word of God *is* the word of God. In our desire to win and hold the attention of the congregation, we must not lose sight of the fact that we are engaged on a sacred task.

There are two dimensions to this task. Karl Barth once famously remarked that preachers should prepare their sermons with the Bible in one hand and a newspaper in the other. John Stott speaks of the preacher being a bridge-builder between two worlds—he or she must stand with one foot in the

Scriptures and the other in the contemporary world.[17] Ian Pitt-Watson, in turn, spoke of this as the calling to expound faithfully two texts—the text of Scripture and the text of life—which share the same author.[18]

In terms of the text of Scripture, those who preach at weddings need to be clear, not just about the meaning of the passage or passages that the couple have chosen for the marriage, but also about the more general teaching of Scripture concerning marriage.

We might also reflect on the changing understanding of marriage in our culture as expressed in film, TV and literature and consider how the Scriptures address and challenge the prevailing assumptions about marriage that they present.

The process of 'invention' needs to be done with some sensitivity to the circumstances of both the couple and their guests. In the course of conversations leading up to the marriage the minister will be learning quite a lot about the jobs, interests and personalities of the couple. There may also be issues such as divorce or bereavement in the extended family that emerge during these discussions that will have some bearing on what is to be said (or not said) at the wedding.

What is needed at this stage of the procedure is a mixture of intellectual rigour and pastoral sensitivity. This is the substructure of the talk—little of it may be explicitly referred to in the actual address, but if there is no clarity in the thinking of the preacher at this stage of preparation, the talk will lack substance and integrity when it is delivered.

Arrangement

This part of the process is about the preacher ordering his or her thoughts into a coherent structure. One immediate question that needs to be addressed here is who the talk is aimed at. Opinions differ as to whether the talk should be primarily addressed to the congregation or to the couple, but it is surely not beyond the realms of possibility to include elements of both. We have already observed the need to reflect on both the text of Scripture and the text of life. The particular personalities and circumstances of the couple getting married will feed into the content of the talk, but they may also provide some clues to the structure.

Sometimes, a job or hobby of the couple may help to provide a structure for the talk. On one occasion, for example, I was asked to speak at the wedding of a friend who was then working for a company that printed bank notes. They had chosen to have Proverbs 31 as their reading, and I used features of a bank note as the pegs on which I hung my talk. From memory, I had an enlarged photocopy of a £10 note (which, on reflection, might have been illegal!) and spoke about the importance of the promise, the marks of authenticity and the image of a 'good lady.'

Whether or not it is possible to base the structure of the talk around some aspect of the couple, it is important to include some connections with them as people that will root the message in the here and now of the marriage of this particular couple.

Style

Clyde Fant memorably refers to two dialects in which preachers are apt to speak, which he calls Upper and Lower Garble. When speaking Upper Garble, the preacher is concerned to appear as clever as possible and will avoid using a short word where a longer word would do. But obscurity should never be confused with profundity—as Spurgeon is said to have observed, many apparently deep preachers are in reality only empty wells! Go through the text of your talk with a red pen and cross out any theological jargon or references that would be meaningless to someone who does not normally attend church!

Fant's second *bête noir* is Lower Garble. This is the dialect adopted by preachers who speak to nobody in particular about nothing in particular. This is a besetting sin of quite a number of preachers who only have one or two ideas, so they keep returning to them. This is not to say that one or two ideas might not be sufficient for a wedding address—what matters is that these ideas have some substance to them.[19]

'You can take a horse to water, but you can't make him drink...but you can put salt in his oats!'

The most effective sermons are like icebergs, with 90% of the weight kept below the surface. This is particularly true in wedding sermons—the 10% that pokes above the water should be intriguing enough to make people wonder if there might be more to the Christian faith than they had previously imagined. It is sometimes asked whether wedding sermons should be evangelistic. I personally doubt if it is often appropriate to be directly evangelistic, but the service as a whole, and the sermon in particular, should be presented in such a way that they commend Christ and elicit interest in the gospel. As a friend of mine once remarked, 'You can take a horse to water, but you can't make him drink...but you can put salt in his oats!' From an evangelistic perspective, the approach I am suggesting is about putting salt in the oats of couple and congregation alike.

Preachers need to be flexible in the way that they present their messages, and a wedding is an occasion that demands a mixture of formality and informality. The intention should be to set people at ease—that you know what you are doing and that they can afford to relax and enjoy, not just endure, the ceremony.

The impression that preachers need to present is that they are serious about what they are doing without being sombre. Humour is one way of achieving this, but Ian Bunting raises a note of caution on this matter. If we use humour, it needs to be done in a way that does not conform to the stereotypical image of the very jolly but utterly vacuous minister.[20] The best guidance is to be yourself—do not *try* to be funny, but be prepared to use humour if it seems natural to do so. If people are unsure, let them know that it is all right to laugh in church. If you are relaxed with the couple and their families, this will help to set the tone—this may well be one of the by-products of the rehearsal beforehand.

Another factor in the consideration of style is the position from which the address is to be delivered. Reference has been made to the fact that the message is most likely to be delivered from the chancel steps rather than the pulpit. This immediately establishes a different relationship between preacher and congregation that means that a somewhat different style of speaking is probably appropriate. It is much easier to build a relationship of this kind when you are physically on the same level, rather than several feet above them.

Those who have been taking weddings for many years may already have developed a style that they never question. It does none of us any harm, however, to reflect on whether the way we do it is the *only* way we could do it, or even the *best* way we could do it. Perhaps we may feel that we could experiment with slightly different styles on different occasions.

Memory

Having discovered what there was to say, how to order the material into a coherent structure and determined the appropriate means of communicating with the given audience, the next task of the public speaker is to make the message memorable, first for the speaker and then for the hearer.

It might be good here to comment about the appropriate length for a wedding talk. I would not want to be dogmatic, but a good rule of thumb seems to be 5–10 minutes. There is generally a lot of goodwill at weddings, which can bear fruit if treated with care and respect. However, an overlong address will dissipate the congregation's goodwill and may unnecessarily alienate them.

Preachers vary in the use they make of notes in their regular preaching, but the more tied to notes you are, the less able you are to engage with the congregation. Notes for a wedding sermon should be minimal—if the preacher cannot remember the direction of their message at the beginning of a wedding talk, there is little prospect that the congregation will be able to at the end!

It sounds redundant to make the point, but one of the aspects of preaching that is most often forgotten, especially by beginners, is that the sermon is an oral event. In a book, headings can be signalled with the use of bold type and numbers, and if the meaning of a sentence is not clear straight away, the reader can glance back at the text and have a second go at it. The congregation has only one chance of catching what is said in a sermon, so it has to be clear at the first hearing, and the structure and progression of the message needs to be communicated verbally.

One tool that many preachers use is a visual aid in the form of a wedding present. Over the years a number of couples have told me that they were presented with a pair of garden shears at their wedding. The talk was then structured around the analogy between marriage and shears—two parts joined together, often moving in different directions and woe betide anyone who comes between them! The more resourceful clergy gave a supplementary gift of a can of Three-in-One oil in order to demonstrate the difference that the Triune God can make to a marriage. I do not know where this talk originated, but each of these couples has been happy to credit their minister with great creativity and have long remembered the point of the sermon.

The fact that people remember these talks for a long time bears out the well-known fact that the visual alongside the oral is educationally far more effective than speech alone.

It might be objected that buying a pair of garden shears two or three times a month could get a little expensive. Where I have given wedding presents I have to confess that they have usually been somewhat less extravagant, but I do believe that they can help to make the sermon memorable—and they often provide a talking point between the couple and their guests for a long time to come. (If you want to use the above idea, you could just as well use a pair of scissors or secateurs!)

Another weapon in the speaker's armoury is the use of the memorable phrase. Skilful politicians make a speciality of it—whoever dreamt up Tony Blair's catchphrase 'Tough on crime, tough on the causes of crime' must be owed a fortune in royalties from the last decade or so. One of my colleagues at Trinity College Bristol preached a memorable sermon at the College's thirtieth anniversary in which he reworked and developed the question 'How much of everything can one person do?' This question was at the centre of the address and remembering it brought back the content of his talk.

The capacity for the wedding address to be remembered has been considerably increased by the advent of videos. Many clergy are defensive about videos, but while still photography can be intrusive, in most churches a video can be taken discreetly. The recording enables those unable to be present to witness the wedding later, and also provides a valuable resource for the couple in the future to remember the vows they made and the words that were spoken.

Perhaps a private aim of the preacher could be to ensure that the couple will not reach for the fast-forward when the video gets to the sermon!

Delivery

Most of what has been thought about so far has concerned the preparation of the message. The focus now turns to the event itself, and, as ever in communication, accurate reception rather than impressive transmission is the ultimate objective.

As a matter of practical logistics, it is now common practice to provide seats for the bride and groom rather than leaving them standing nose to nose with the minister at the chancel steps. If at all possible, the seats should be arranged so that the preacher and anyone else taking part in the service (for example, reading a lesson or taking the prayers) can have eye contact both with the bride and groom and with the congregation.

Delivery was another aspect of rhetoric which received considerable attention in the training and development of public speakers in the ancient world, but which is regarded in many circles today as almost too sordid to deal with.

We have already noted the lessons that can be learnt from the way that skilful politicians craft their speeches, and we can also learn from other professional public speakers. Whatever decision we come to about the use of humour, there is a surprising amount that can be gleaned from a careful study of stand-up comedians. David Day devotes a whole chapter of his excellent book to this topic, drawing out the way in which comedians use a range of skills to develop a relationship with their audiences. Day draws attention to the way in which comedians like Jasper Carrott and Billy Connolly dwell on stories—especially those with human interest—use their observational skills to notice the quirky and unusual things about daily life, understand and respond to their audience, introduce visual elements through word pictures, facial expressions and gestures, and, of course, are masters of timing! All of these skills, like those of David Beckham, are natural gifts that have been refined and developed through hard work and training.[21] Rory Bremner's increasingly political satire is an example of the way that comedy can be used as a powerful tool by someone with a clear message to communicate.

The need to create a relationship with the congregation is true for all preaching, but it is *especially* true for the wedding sermon. People have come principally to see the couple married, not to listen to a lecture. They are not generally hostile to a sermon being preached, but they need to be persuaded in the first few moments of the talk that the preacher has something worthwhile to contribute to the occasion, and to a certain extent they will take their cue from the preacher. If the preacher projects the sense that they have something important to say and that this message fits naturally into the proceedings, then the chances are that people will at least give them the benefit of the doubt and start off listening reasonably attentively.

Related to the issue of style is another concern for the ancient rhetoricians, that of *ethos*. This refers to the sense of congruence between the preacher's public and private persona—the preacher who becomes a different person when they launch into their sermons will find that the dissonance created will damage the effectiveness of their preaching. There is an issue of integrity here for any preacher, but for those who are rooted in a specific community it is more than a private concern—the pastor who is known to be at odds with his or her spouse will find it hard to carry conviction if they present a rose-tinted vision of marital harmony.

In situations where the preacher is also the minister conducting the service, some relationship with the congregation will already have been established before the start of the address, so there should be a relatively seamless transition. (I rarely begin a wedding address with a prayer, as I hope that people will already have been learning from the teaching implicit in the liturgy of the service).

The situation is slightly different for someone who has been asked to preach at a service alongside another minister who is conducting the ceremony. In this case some thought needs to be given to establishing the preacher's place in the proceedings. It will help if the preacher is well introduced by the colleague, with an explanation of any relationship that the preacher has with the couple: 'We are very pleased to welcome the Revd Matilda Cox, who is the Vicar of All Saints and a long-standing friend of Jane and Alistair…' This at least gives the congregation some clue as to why another person has stepped up to the plate. If no one else does it for you, take the initiative and introduce yourself!

The preacher will bring to the message something timeless—the message of a loving God who has gifted us marriage in creation and also offers us a personal relationship with himself through Christ. There will also be something fresh about the message—something adapted to the circumstances of this particular marriage. As we have observed, there is nothing wrong in using the ideas of other preachers and writers. A word of caution does need to be mentioned with regard to the final element of the old adage. While humour has its place in the way the service is conducted and the sermon delivered, something has gone seriously wrong when the preacher draws on the same sources of material as the worst kind of best man's speeches. Something old, something new, something borrowed, but, please, nothing blue! In an attempt to be 'relevant,' do not make the mistake of overstepping the lines of decency.

6

Some Ideas Based on Specific Readings

Common Worship offers 22 suggested readings (including one from the Apocrypha) and four Psalms in its Supplementary Texts section of the Marriage Service.

This is somewhat less than the 64 suitable readings listed by Ian Bunting, which should serve as a reminder that the suggestions in *Common Worship* are not exhaustive!

Christian couples who are familiar with the Scriptures sometimes come up with some surprising and original choices, and this can come as a refreshing change to the preacher used to dealing only with 1 Corinthians 13! For other couples the task of choosing a biblical reading can seem quite daunting, and we have found it helpful to offer them a small booklet containing the text of the *Common Worship* readings, which at least gives them a starting point. This is reasonably easy to produce, as the text can be copied either from the Church of England web site or from Visual Liturgy.

When the couple have chosen the reading, I offer to forward to them an email with the text of the passage so that they can reproduce it in their Order of Service. This means that guests are likely to be more attentive to the Scriptures when they are being read and gives the preacher the opportunity to refer to the text during the address.

Song of Songs 2.10–13; 8.6–7

This is probably the most creative choice in the new service book, and has already proved to be very popular with couples I have married in recent years.

The Song of Songs uses poetry and euphemism to describe the developing love between a man and a woman. It is the evocative quality of the writing that generally attracts people towards this reading, but unlike many sentimental pieces of secular literature that couples often chose, the two excerpts from the Song of Songs selected by the compilers of *Common Worship* provide the preacher with some great material for a sermon. The following could be the framework for an address between the Declarations and the Vows.

I wonder if it has ever struck you how strange love is. Two people grow up in loving homes, perfectly happy with their mum and dad, and reasonably happy with their brothers and sisters, and before you know where you are, they are wanting to exchange the security of what they know to set up a new relationship with someone they have only known for a few years. *(This could be added to with material relevant to the couple).*

It is certainly a day to remember—and I want to offer you a gift that I hope will help you to remember it each and every day of your future life together. *(Present a hinged photograph frame capable of taking two photographs).*

There's nothing new about what is happening to Roy and Emma—it has been going on for generations—and it is the theme of the reading that they have chosen. Before they go any further, perhaps it would be a good idea to look at that reading.

The first thing to say is that the reading is taken from the Song of Songs, which is probably the most *risqué* book in the Bible. It is an unashamed celebration of the love of a man and woman and the reading that we have just heard is actually in two parts.

The first part of the reading comes near the beginning of the book and represents the beginning of the relationship. Emma—or somebody like her—is at home with mum and dad, when Roy—or somebody like him—comes leaning over the front wall and peering through the window. It's spring time, the flowers are in blossom and he suggests, with a degree of urgency, that she might like to come out for a walk with him. He makes her an offer she can't resist, and away they go.

Time passes, and I'll leave you to read on your own what else passes, until we get to the final section of the reading.

The final words are pretty dramatic *(read verse 7)*. The mention of water and fire is a reminder of the reality that all love is tested by the ups and downs of life. Seeing what lies ahead, the girl asks two things of her man: 'Set me as a seal upon your heart, as a seal upon your arm.'

A seal is a sign of belonging—and she wants to know that when they are apart or facing difficult circumstances that their relationship will be strong enough to depend upon.

She wants to be set as a seal upon his heart. This is the private side of their relationship—the trust and intimacy that is between them and the commitment to place the welfare of that relationship above the temptations of personal pleasure or convenience. In the next few hours many pictures are going to be taken of you both—I would like to invite you to choose the most romantic of them and place it in the frame to the left.

In the other part of the frame I would like you to place a photo of the two of you surrounded by your family and friends as a reminder of the other part of this verse—the seal on the arm. Actually it is hard to tell from the original whether this seal is on the arm or the finger—and some people suggest that the word used for seal could refer to the way that animals are branded. There is something both public and permanent about it. And that is what is special about today.

The commitment that you are about to make to each other involves everybody here. Your family and friends have already pledged to 'support and uphold you in your marriage now and in the years to come.'

You will make promises to each other that will provide security whether you are together or apart, in the midst of happy times or testing times. You need to look at the photo of each other and know that it represents the gift of trust that must be honoured. You will make those promises in the presence of friends and family, who will be there to support you and help you—again there is a gift of trust between you and them that must be honoured. But there is also a third dimension. The writer speaks of love as being like a raging flame. It is a hard word to translate—one writer calls it a 'fierce and holy blaze'; another says it is an 'almighty great flame.' The word contains the name of God—who provides the strength and intensity of the flame.

What has drawn you together is a love that is a gift of the Creator. As you make your commitment today, as you seek to honour the trust that you have placed in one another, you are fulfilling the purposes of the one whom we can trust above all.

1 Corinthians 13

Still number one in the all-time top ten wedding readings, this is one of the readings, along with Colossians 3.12–17, that connects most closely with the model of marriage discussed in chapter 4.

A wedding is not the occasion to attempt exhaustive exposition. I am sure that some preachers would find enough material in this chapter to keep them going for many months, so we will have to be selective. I have generally used the image of love in three dimensions when speaking from this passage, and have sometimes used a gift related to the couple's profession. Sometimes I have given something clearly three dimensional.

Peter, Sally, congratulations! This is a great day and you have chosen a great passage to be read today. It is probably one of the best known chapters in the Bible, and it is a wonderful celebration of love.

Now love is a much misused term. We can all tell from your faces that you are in love, but that wasn't the question I asked you a few moments ago. I didn't ask you, Peter, if you were in love with Sally. I asked will you love her. You have made the decision that you will love each other and I want to spend a few moments now exploring what that means.

The passage you have chosen comes from a letter written by a man named Paul, who knew a great deal about love. I want to think about the three dimensions in which this passage suggests that love operates.

First of all, love deals with the past. Paul says that love keeps no record of wrongs. One friend of mine suggests that the motto of every marriage should be 'Never say never again!' It seems a strange suggestion, but what it means is that we have to learn to both forgive and forget. When we say something like 'You never put the lid back on the toothpaste' we are really saying that there are lots of past offences that we are always ready to dredge up and confront our partner with.

True love deals with the past. It means that we are able to say sorry, forgive and move on. It is one of the most liberating of all human experiences.

The second dimension is the present. Love equips us in the present.

Peter and Sally look very relaxed now, but we had some interesting moments at the rehearsal (*recount some, if there were any*). Sally was nothing like as nervous as one bride I heard of. She was so worried that she lay in bed running through the first few minutes of the service. 'I walk up the aisle, stop at the altar and then we sing the first hymn.' Aisle, altar, hymn. (*Say this a couple of times, first slowly and distinctly and then running the words together: 'I'll alter him'*).

That is the problem with many relationships. We find it difficult to accept each other as we are, and we think that we can change our partners to fit the images that we have created of them.

But Paul says 'Love is patient, love is kind.' These are two sides of the way love responds to others. Patience is translated in old versions of the Bible as 'long suffering'—it basically means that we are willing to accept our partner's weaknesses as well as their strengths. Kindness is an active word. It means thinking of practical things that we can do to help or please our partner—and then doing them!

In your vows, you committed yourself to one another 'for better, for worse; for richer, for poorer; in sickness and in health.' This kind of commitment provides great security, whatever the circumstances life may bring. It will only be a reality if you discover the disciplines of patience and kindness.

So two down, one to go (*relating to the visual aid, or gift*). True love deals with the past; true love equips us in the present and true love prepares us for the future.

Some people will have said to you that they hope today is the happiest day of your lives. Can I sincerely say that I hope it isn't! I hope it is a wonderful day, that you will look back on with great joy, but if it is the happiest day of your life, it is all down hill from now on!

True love has a vision of the future, a belief that the best is yet to be. Paul had that confidence. Love always trusts, always hopes, always perseveres. You are beginning a life-time adventure together and if you learn to let love deal with the past and equip you for the present then you can look forward to the future with confidence and hope.

Sometimes this passage is made to sound like sentimental idealism. For Paul it was practical, real and true. He had encountered this kind of love for himself in his relationship with Jesus. This gave him a confidence that reached beyond this life into the next. He looks forward to the day when he will see Jesus face to face.

Peter and Sally, as you set off on this journey of marriage, I hope that you will discover true love in all its dimensions—in each other, but also in the one in whom Paul saw it most clearly, the God who is both the source and the model of love.

Appendix

Some Suggested Readings

Those not included in the *Common Worship* Marriage Service are in italic type.[22]

Old Testament and Apocrypha	New Testament
Genesis 1.26–28	Matthew 5.1–10
Genesis 2.18–24 (or 25)	Matthew 7.21; 24–29
Ruth 1:16–18	*Matthew 19.3–6*
Psalm 67	*Matthew 22.24–40*
Psalm 121	Mark 10.6–9; 13–16
Psalm 127	John 2.1–11
Psalm 128	John 15.1–8
Proverbs 31.10–31	John 15.9–17
Ecclesiastes 4.9–12	Romans 7.1–2; 9–18
Song of Solomon 2.10–13; 8.6–7	Romans 8.31–35; 37–39
Jeremiah 31.31–34	Romans 12.1–2; 9–13
Tobit 8.4–8	Romans 15.1–3, 5–7; 13
	1 Corinthians 13.1–13
	Ephesians 3.14–21
	Ephesians 4.1–6
	Ephesians 4.25–5.2
	Ephesians 5.21–33
	Philippians 4.4–9
	Colossians 3.12–17
	1 Peter 3.1–9
	1 John 3.18–24
	1 John 4.7–12
	Revelation 19.1, 5–9

Notes

1. Thomas Cranmer produced the first English language Prayer Book in 1549, subsequently revised in 1552. The *Book of Common Prayer*, drawing substantially on Cranmer's work, was published in 1662. The first major period of modern liturgical reform culminated in the production of a new Prayer Book in 1928, but the House of Commons refused to authorize its use. The Marriage Service from this book was finally authorized in 1966 as part of the 'Series One' set of liturgy, a status it still retains. The *Alternative Service Book* (ASB) followed in 1980 and Common Worship in 2000.

2. Ian Bunting, *Preaching at Weddings* (Grove Worship booklet, W 74) p 5.

3. The *Office for National Statistics* is the source of the data given in the following paragraphs. These are available free of charge online and regularly updated. http://www.statistics.gov.uk

4. Wesley Carr, *Brief Encounters* (London: SPCK, 1985) p 88.

5. *Marriages Abroad*, Government Actuaries Department, http://www.gad.gov.uk/marital_status_projections/2003/marriages_abroad.htm

6. See *The Death of Christian Britain (Christianity & Society in the Modern World)*, (Routledge, 2000).

7. *Cohabitation in Great Britain: past, present and future trends—and attitudes*, Population Trends, Spring 2001, produced by the Office for National Statistics.

8. Also taken from Population Trends. This figure relates to 1992.

9. *Living in Britain 2002*. Available at the National Statistics website.

10. See Charles Read and Anna de Lange, *Common Worship Marriage* (Grove Worship booklet, W 162) p 4.

11. The Office for National Statistics. See *Marriage in Church after Divorce* (London: Church House Publishing, 2000) Appendix 4.

12. The five key points are: the new relationship must not have been a factor in the breakdown of a previous marriage; the divorced person or persons must have come to a mature understanding of the breakdown of their previous marriages; they should be at a place where they have worked through the sense of conflict in their previous relationships and be able to offer forgiveness to their former partners; they should recognize that divorce is a breach of God's intention for marriage; adequate financial and emotional support should be provided to any children of previous marriages. For further details, see *Marriage in Church after Divorce* (London: Church House Publishing, 2003).

13. *Common Worship: Pastoral Services* (London: Church House Publishing, 2000) p 105.

14. 'The Fourme of Solemnizacyon of Matrymonye' in the 1552 *Book of Common Prayer*.

15. *De Bono Coniugali*. Augustine (354–430) was Bishop of Hippo in North Africa.

16. The Balswicks develop this idea in a number of places, but see particularly *The Family* (Grand Rapids: Baker, 1997).

17. See John Stott, *I Believe in Preaching* (London: Hodder, 1982) chapter 4. The American version of this book was actually called *Between Two Worlds*.

18. See *A Primer for Preachers* (Grand Rapids: Baker Book House, 1986). This book, written by an exceptional preacher, is one of the best introductions to the subject.

19. See *Preaching for Today* (New York: Harper and Row, 1975) chapter 10.

20. Ian Bunting, *Preaching at Weddings* (Grove Worship booklet, W 74) p 7.

21. See David Day, *A Preaching Workbook* (London: SPCK, 1998) chapter 6.

22. See *Common Worship: Pastoral Services* (London: Church House Publishing, 2000) pp 137–149.